The Dog
Ate My Homework

The Dog
Ate My Homework

Poems by Sara Holbrook

Boyds Mills Press

To my teacher, Lyle Crist,
for making me cut it in half.
And again.

Published by Wordsong
Boyds Mills Press, Inc.
A Highlights Company
815 Church Street
Honesdale, Pennsylvania 18431
Printed in the United States of America

Publisher Cataloging-in-Publication Data
Holbrook, Sara.
The dog ate my homework / by Sara Holbrook.—2nd ed.
Revised edition.
[48]p. ; cm.
Summary : A collection of poems about school.
ISBN 1-56397-638-2
1. Schools—Juvenile Poetry. 2. Children's Poetry, American.
[1. Schools—Poetry. 2. American poetry.] I. Title.
811.54—dc20 1996 AC CIP
Library of Congress Catalog Card Number 96-85177

Second edition, 1996
Book designed by Tim Gillner
Cover concept and photography by The Reuben Group
The text of this book is set in 12-point Berkeley.

10 9 8 7 6

Table of Contents

I CAN'T

I can't have cake for breakfast?
No Popsicles?
No gum?
No root beer floats?
No chocolate chips?
No candy bars?
How come?

No soda pop?
Or ice cream?

Just like in the past.
I never get the good stuff.
I just thought I'd ask.

NO TIME

I can't brush my teeth.
It's eight-twenty-eight.
Get out of my face,
I'm gonna be late.
Into the bathroom?
Have you checked the time?
I don't smell like horse breath.
My tongue tastes just fine.
You act like they're yours,
but my molars are mine.
I'm so mad at your ordering
all of the time.
Just once in a while,
if I only could win,
I'd laugh and applaud
with a big, toothless grin.
Okay.
So okay.
I'll brush if you'll quit.
I'm warning you now, though,

there's no time to spit.

SWIMMING UPSTREAM

Why am I late for school?
Why don't I have a note?
My umbrella got infected
and threw up all its spokes.
Look at me.
I'm soaked.

My legs are like two waterfalls.
My sneakers ate my socks.
I put my bookbag on my head
and had to swim the last two blocks.

I was a dedicated salmon.
I came upstream, against the flow.
And when my whole life flashed before me?
I bravely fought the undertow.

I need a medal, not a note!
Just look what I survived.
I deserve some extra credit.
I am here.
And I'm alive.

THE DOG ATE MY HOMEWORK

The dog ate my homework.
You've heard that before?
This one ate the table,
then chewed through the door.

Broke into the living room
with his munch mouth,
snacked on some carpet,
and lunched on the couch.

He chewed up some albums,
then swallowed the mail,
even ate pretzels,
'though they were stale.

He garbaged down everything
left in his path
and still wasn't full
when he found my math.

He chewed tops off bottles
then drank all the pop.
As far as I know,
he still hasn't stopped.

If you don't believe me,
then give Mom a call,
if she still has a kitchen
or phone on the wall.

She'll answer and tell you
my story is true.
The dog ate my homework.
What could I do?

MY CAREER PATH

I filled my sister's blow-up pool,
stood up on the garage.
I like to see my mother faint.
I hollered, "Hey, Mom, watch!"

I jumped out of the dryer once
and scared her into tears,
then drugged the cat with nasal spray.
She grounded me for years.

I crazy-glued the ironing board
to my mother's blouse.
Sprayed water in the fuse box
and shorted out the house.

She couldn't wait till fall,
so she could pack the pool,
put a sandwich in my lunchbox
and bus me off to school.

I can't sit where I'm told,
of course.
I'd rather dance or stand.
I booby-trapped the teacher's desk.
Walked the window sill, no hands.

I'd say that I'm adventurous.
Born with brains and guts,
full speed down my career path:

DRIVING GROWN-UPS NUTS!

WHAT'S THE POINT?

What is the purpose in existing?
Why am I alive?
Answers I was searching for
in my closet at 8:05.
It was just a normal morning,
undercovered, overslept.
Alarmed into racing around —
I wasn't looking where I stepped.

How do trees recover from winter?
How do birds find their way?
Has the sun ever been grounded?
What's the meaning of today?

School should answer certain questions,
like, why's the ocean blue?
Who invented morning?
And
why'd the cat throw up in my shoe?

THE SEARCH

"X" makes my tongue itch
and squirms my insides,
my teeth chew my nails
and my throat starts to cry.

My mouth has no spit,
and I'm falling behind.
Where is that dumb quotient
that I'm s'posed to find?

I'm in math overload.
If I don't find that "X" soon
my brain will explode
like a water balloon.

STUCK HERE

Today's lesson is on gravity.

If there weren't such a thing as gravity,
my feet wouldn't stick to the floor.
Instead I would rise like a stone
and fly like a pig through the door.

Open your books to page 138.

I could hit baseballs out of the park,
but I couldn't play soccer or bowl.
I guess I could maybe still rock,
but for sure I couldn't roll.

John will you begin reading for us?

I could up-and-over-slam-dunk a house.
I could vault without a pole.
I could plow through clouds in the sky
or I could fall up a hole.
I'd just need cruise control.

John?

“This is the flying Titanic to ground control.”
Accelerating—picking up speed . . .
destination, the South Pole.
“You’re fading on me. Do you read?”

Mr. Beasley. Is your mind on gravity?
Let’s just stick to the book, Mr. Beasley.

Gravity is heavy,
and you can bet that it’s for real.
Look how I’m stuck to this book.
Gravity.
Bum deal.

NOTHING TO LOSE

My pen took a walk,
my notes got confused,
my book stayed at home.
What more could I lose?

I might as well croak,
I have no excuse.
No way to avoid it,
I'm in for abuse.

SPELLBOUND

Confluence
and recompense,
aphid,
ibex,
muse,
chrysalis and zygote.
Words
I know I'll never use.
But like
gossamer and quell,
I had to learn to spell.

GYM

I showered,
like you said.
You think I'm some dope?
It's your fault
if you didn't
tell me,
"Use soap."

HISTORY

History is to Mr. Lee
  what peanut butter is to me.
Lee feeds all day on his paper stack
  with chalky dates stuck on his back.

He always bites off more than he's planned
  then tries to talk and we can't understand.
He wouldn't be bad, just a naptime bore,
  if his breath didn't smell like the Civil War.

He knows more than I'll ever know
  and he's STILL eating facts to make him grow.
Lee's bald at the top and wide at the seat.
  Living proof—you are what you eat.

SPUNK BIT CHRISTINE

Spunk bit Christine.
Did it have to be her?
With all her dramatics,
she'll kick up a stir.

I'm finished, you know.
She'll demand plastic surgery.
Though I'm not without friends,
you can bet they'll all turn on me.

She'll start up some rumors,
get kids on her side.
My life's in the trash
'cause of this gerbil bite.

Can you picture the playground?
No one will swing.
They'll all hang on her
with her arm in a sling.

She'll moan and she'll groan,
or squeak out a cry.
I'm expecting real tears,
or at least her best try.

She'll probably have crutches,
just for effect.
Spunk bit the school actress!
My whole life is wrecked.

MY DESK

If my desk weren't such a mess,
I could find my organizer.
If my desk weren't such a mess
I'd be quicker, smarter, wiser.

Picture an abyss,
bottomless and black,
jammed and overflowing,
inkless pens and wrinkled stacks
of papers (uncompleted),
candy wrappers,
salad tossed with
petrifying carrots,
leaking glue and
what-got-lost.

It's hard to stay on task
when tasks are buried six-feet-deep.
I'm always playing catch-up,
overdue and underneat.

Honor Roll won't happen
while I'm squirreling through this mess.
But if this desk were neat and straight,
well then,
it wouldn't be my desk.

FAST MOVES

Cooties.
Gobbers.
Sinko.
Dread.
Alison got kissed by Fred.
He caught her squarely on the lips,
then puckered up and let 'er rip.

Then, Fred-the-Lip?
He strut and bragged.
And Alison?
She spat and gagged.

Fred's a rookie,
didn't ask for permission.
Should have known that in kissing,
you play your position.

If he tries it again,
he may get a new twist
from the school's brand new nickname . . .
Alison-the-Fist.

DISCHARGED IN CLASS

In class,
it chortled softly in my pocket,
secret sounds
I couldn't understand.
I was so careful when I moved,
patting it gently with my hand.

When out of the quiet
it clean-jerked,
croaked
and bolted.
The room went off—
a box of screaming fireworks.

I swear.
I didn't know
the frog was loaded.

BAD WORDS

Sammy knows bad words,
he uses them to fight.
He knows about a hundred swears,
and how to use 'em right.

I don't know where he learned
how to talk that way,
with words that have a sting
but don't have much to say.

FIGHTING WORDS

A fight is like an infection,
it just gets passed along,
with most people
catching the anger
before they know who's wrong.

Friends start choosing sides,
exchanging picks and nudges,
causing us to hurt
and making lasting scars
called grudges.

CALL-BACKS

Okay.
I said,
"You are a pigface,"
'cause I wanted to be mean.

I said,
"You'll never need a costume
when it comes to Halloween."

I said,
"You are a dip brain
with a twisted attitude."

I said
that no one likes you,
which I guess was pretty rude.

Words are automatic weapons
and I fired the first name.
It isn't easy to admit it,
but this time I'm to blame.

I didn't aim to kill,
I want our friendship
back on track.
I could have made it worse,
I could have talked
behind your back.

Okay.
When I said,
"You are a cockroach,"
it wasn't to be kind.
But don't stay mad forever.
My anger changed its mind.

BORED WITH CONSEQUENCES

There's no one now to bike with
or hang out at the pool.
Randy had a fist fight
yesterday in school.

I don't know what started it,
he can't remember either.
How was he supposed to know
that new kid was a bleeder?

Two weeks in his bedroom.
Isn't this just dandy?
I feel cheated and depressed.
Who's grounded?
Me?
Or Randy?

REVENGE

I asked her to sleep over.
Boy, was that move dumb.
She couldn't wait till Monday
to tell I sucked my thumb.

She told them in the bathroom.
Of course they laughed at me.
I'm hating her forever,
and when we're twenty-three?

I'll walk up to her boyfriend,
who may think she's cool,
until he hears she wet her pants
walking home from school.

GAMES

I want contacts, red hair,
and ten pounds less of me by Friday.
Wouldn't you say
that way
he'd be jealous and so sorry
that he
dumped me
for Megan who is ugly,
knock-kneed,
and dumber than a pencil?

I still
hope he'll
change and be a nice guy
if I
just try
harder to be pretty.
Still, he
would be
jerky.

Geez, I hate this game.
I guess I'll stay the same.

FAMOUS

The popular crowd
crams up,
like toe jam in the hall,
familiar-elbow-brushing
while I walk against this wall.

Anonymous for now
doesn't bother me.
I know that popular can change
and that fame is always fleet.

Because,
remember last September?
And the jump rope marathon?
And everyone wanted to be
just like that bonehead Jonathon?

These days, who even knows his name?
I mean, the kid peaked out at eight.
If it's not my turn for famous now,
that's okay.
I'll wait.
And save myself for
GREAT!

ONE AND TWO MAKE THREE

If One and Two
and me make three.
And One and Two
get chum-chummy,
then One may think
that three's a crowd
and I could be
the one left out.

I could get my feelings hurt.
Slam a door, kick the cat.
Pout or swear
or turn my back.
I could throw
a mean insult,
'cause three is
just plain difficult.

I could spit
in that One's eye,
or ask,
"How 'bout another try?"

YOU PROMISED

I gave you private thoughts
to hold.
You promised not to tell.
You told.
I trusted friendship
like a bank.
Now they know;
I've you to thank.

When secrets have
my name on them,
don't pass them out
to her or him.
My secrets are a loan
to be
returned upon request
to me.

MISTRUST

What truth wraps up,
mistrust unties.

You can't hold
your friends
in a pack
with
lies.

PRIVATE PARTS

You read MY journal?
Off MY shelf?
MY dreams placed undercover?
Conversations with MYself?

That's where I get to yell
and no one's yelling back.
Where I reach my hand out
and know it won't get smacked.

That's where I go for confidence.
Where I can practice and rehearse.
My spot out of the spotlight.
Where no one tells me not to curse.

I thought I was playing safely.
You peeped!
It's where my thoughts reside.
You thief.
You should have knocked
and let me dress and come outside.

TEACHING TEACHERS

I'm famous
in my kitchen.
I'm famous
on my block.
I'm famous
to my mom.
Go ahead and mock.

You've memorized a lot of names
of people famous in a book.
But I am famous, too.
And I'm for real,
so take a look.

WINTER

Winter paces,
roars and
creeps.
Curls in corners,
oversleeps.

It stalks like a lion,
a seasonal bummer.
Let's hit the fast forward
and press "STOP"
at summer.

WHAT BREAKS

Spring break?
Not really.
That's the time I take my pieces,
humpty-dumpty style,
a week of school release,
to patch up for a while.

I was frosted by the winter
and its darkened,
wind-chilled presence.
I want to warm up
to the sun instead
of basking in fluorescence.

It's cold that leaves me cracked
and worried if and when
spring will come
and put me back together
till I am whole
again.

GETTING GRADED

Opened at school
or
opened at home,
report cards
should be private.
No one else should see
or ask,
"Hey, what'd you get?"

I just hold my breath
and peek
and hardly pout or boast.
Just to know is a relief.
I did my best . . .

almost.

COMMENTS

More than the answers,
it's the questions you ask
that earn
"Satisfactory progress in class."
Teachers like the attention
so remember to mention
some fact from last week,
but don't act like a geek.
If you brown-nose, it shows.

When they sneeze
you can bless.
Laugh when they joke
and smile when you guess.

Remember.
No classroom movement is
"Showing improvement."
But, misplace a pencil,
you're
"Not up to potential."

KIDNAPPED

I meant to do my homework
and should have been beware,
'cause while I wasn't watching
I was kidnapped in that chair.

I would've done those problems,
but have some sympathy,
before I could escape
the dirty crook robbed me.

I'm not some careless chump
who just misplaced the day.
The TV bandit came
and stole my time away.

TWO MORE DAYS

Two more days of school,
of lockers slamming in the hall,
of "class please find your seat,"
and "turn your chairs to the back wall."

Then, no more
who sat where at lunch,
no more giggles by the bunch.
No more watching Wilma's wiggle
when she writes up on the board.
No more trying to look interested
when classes are a snore.

I can't wait!
To go without a pass
and not count seconds till the bell.
No more hunting for a pen
or hearing stressed-out teachers yell
at some poor slob who just forgot
where he was s'posed to be.
No more handing out detentions,
especially not to me.

When summer gets real boring,
I'll be ready to come back.
But now,
two days is two too much.
If it were three —
I'd crack.

WINNERS

I thought they had
something I lacked.
Until I learned,
winners fight back.

It isn't that
they never lose,
don't fall apart
or take abuse.

The trick is,
simply,
every round,
when they get hit?
Winners
don't stay down.